Bipolarism

Medha Sharma

(Medoll)

BookLeaf Publishing

India | USA | UK

Presentation by *BookLeaf Publishing*

Web: www.bookleafpub.com

E-mail: info@bookleafpub.com

ISBN:9789363310841

First edition 2024

DEDICATION

To all those who have ever felt lost in the darkness, this book is for you. May these words serve as a reminder that you are not alone, and that there is always hope, even in the bleakest of times. This book is dedicated to the resilient spirit that lies within each and every one of us, guiding us towards the light even when the path seems obscured. This book is also dedicated to the all the volunteers who have worked with me in Silly Opera, a beautiful community to advocate and empower communications around mental health.

ACKNOWLEDGEMENT

To my friends and family, thank you for your
unwavering love and encouragement, even
during my darkest moments, which I never
confronted. Your understanding and empathy
have given me the courage to continue on this
path of self-expression.
To Shivedita Singh, with whom I built the
beautiful community Silly Opera, I owe heartfelt
gratitude. Together, we envisioned a safe haven
for those suffering in silence, providing hope
and a space for open conversations about mental
health and emotions. Thank you for helping
create 'SomeoneWhoListens.'
To that one long-distance friend I lost, who
taught me that life is a gift as is, surviving is
already an achievement, and living should be
continued to all that is yet to come.
I am deeply grateful to myself for
single-handedly supporting me on my own
journey towards self-discovery and healing.

To my readers, thank you for allowing me to
share my story with you. And to the universe,
thank you for teaching me resilience in the face
of adversity.

PREFACE

In the pages of "Bipolarism," I invite you to join me on a journey through the labyrinth of my mind. These poems are a reflection of my innermost struggles with social anxiety and depression, written during a time when I felt lost and alone. Through the darkness, I discovered the power of poetry as a means of self-expression and healing. Each verse is a raw and unfiltered portrayal of my journey towards self-discovery and acceptance. May these words serve as a beacon of hope for those who find themselves navigating similar paths.

Whispers of Resilience

Beneath the shadowed sun, I stand,
Dreams flicker in this desolate land.
In the night, stars gleam, so far,
Yet with you, I see hope's soft star.

Journeying to the sunrise sea,
Yearning for eternity.
Heavy rain, city's somber song,
Yet within, dreams carry along.

Falling, weightless in the sky,
Days pass, yet dreams refuse to die.
Your words, a lifeline in the dark,
Guiding toward a distant spark.

Each moment a struggle, pain's cruel test,
Yet through it all, dreams persist.
From the ache of beginnings to the end's faint
gleam,
Chasing dreams, a solitary dream.

~Medoll

I want to fly

Even if I die, I want to fly.

I am incapable
I have no skill
I am good but not enough
I am under that bridge of talent
No matter what you say to me.
I don't believe, he is better than me.
Even if I die, I want to fly.

~Medoll

Starry canvas

In the quiet hush of starlit skies,
A dreamer's fervor begins to rise.
Her efforts, like sparks, ignite the night,
Yet unseen by those blinded by daylight's light.

But when she departs, to realms afar,
Her legacy shines like a radiant star.
Cut her out and scattered like little lights,
Her passion, her art, her endless fights.

For in the heavens, her face shall gleam,
A tapestry of dreams, a cosmic dream.
And all the world, in love with the night,
Will see her brilliance, her wondrous light.

Though in life, her struggles were unknown,
In death, her brilliance is fully shown.
A testament to her undying flame,
In the starry canvas, she etches her name.

~Medoll

Living on Thoughts of

I live on the thoughts of being dead
That's how life has turned me mad
Idling my body I keep on imagining
Different dreadful scenes keep on piling
I live on the thoughts of being dead

"Go out there" will be too much to ask
I'd rather be quiet and put on a mask
"On the stage put an outstanding show"
It'd be a miracle if I survive standing in the last
row
I live on the thoughts of being dead

The feeling of being always misunderstood
Being cornered, questioned and blaming my
mood
Left me choking on the depressing air
On the frozen floor, my feet were bare.
I live on the thoughts of being dead

Words, as sunshine, gave me hope
Some tunes, like a child's fingers, grabbed my
robe
A voice, sweet and sharp, struck a high note
Those eyes, blue with green tint, I dote

I lived on the thoughts of being dead
I, now, will live on the thoughts of being alive!

~Medoll

Cosmos Bloom

12

In the garden of life, you stand tall,
A cosmos flower awaiting its call.
Though spring may pass, and petals may wilt,
In the embrace of time, your dreams will be built.

Wait patiently for autumn's call,
For in its embrace, you'll stand in awe.
Your bloom, destined to unfold gracefully,
A symphony of resilience, so beautifully.

Though setbacks may shadow and doubts may loom,
Your time will come, dispelling all gloom.
Keep faith in the promise of tomorrow's light,
For in the dance of seasons, your glory takes flight.

~Medoll

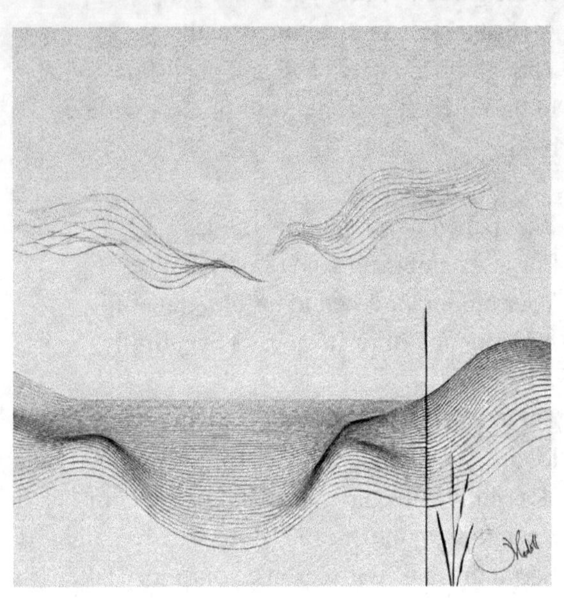

Silent Echoes

Why the urge for my voice to rise?
I can write, I can surmise.
Why this need for spoken word?
I'd rather write, explore the unheard.

To find, to seek, to wander deep,
But to speak? It's not what I keep.
My mind brims with queries vast,
Yet, silence seems to suit me best.

Answers poised upon my tongue,
Yet speech remains unsung.
To shape history, forge theories bold,
Yet still, the need for words remains untold.

Why this push for verbal tale?
To define, to justify, to unveil.
Within me, dreams take flight,
As real as any beating light.

I stand tall, despite my falls,
Yet still, the insistence calls.
To shout, to scream, to break free,
But why this push to hear from me?

~Medoll

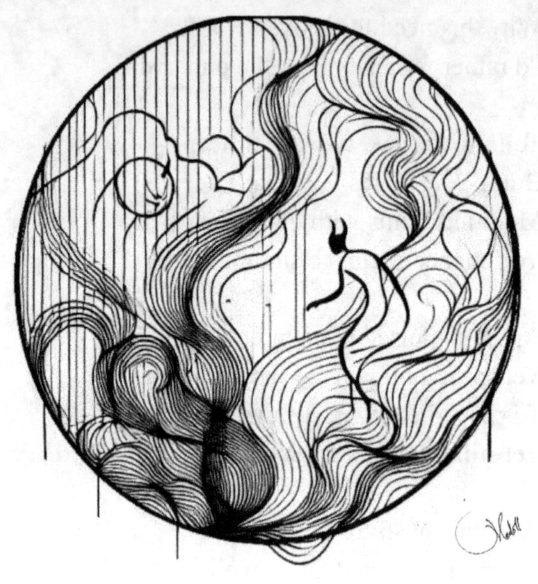

Entrapped soul

I built my own walls
Entrapping my own soul
Mind and heart.
Please, don't push it today.
I may suffocate one day
Running out of breath inside
But let me breathe one more day
Please, don't push it further today.

I have seen the devils of the world
Feasting on my flesh and others'
Scared, I ran and hid my own self
Inside these walls.
They protected me so well—
At least I thought so
Some nerves started to protest
Against the storm that started to emerge
Inside my very own.
I have seen the demons,
The dementors feeding on my soul.
Will I be left here to rot?

Do I have to free myself?
Or wait here for Morpheus
To come and save me

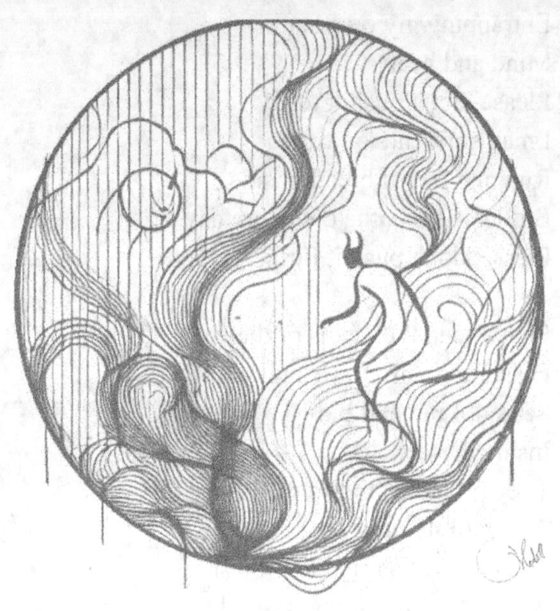

And take me to a place
Where I'm free forever
With no devils or demons altogether.

~Medoll

Come back to life

I whispered
In my
Very own
breath, if
It's hard
Finding your
Purpose of
Your life
Here on
Earth and
If you
Can't be
Prudent enough
Or
Work hard
Yet still
Wonder why
It feels empty
Lonely inside
Then perhaps...
Just die
And never
Come back
To life
Ever again.
      ~Medoll

Oh Snow

Oh Snow! Oh Snow!
So white, so pure.
Dropped on my palm
From the sky,
How can I be calm
On this winter night.
How much I longed
To look at you
One more time
How much I desire
To hold you close.
How much I hoped
Dancing on toes,
Embracing your soul.
Oh snow! oh snow!
You are still so cold
How much I wish
To give you my warmth
But how can I forget?
Why am I a fool?
With my touch,
You can't survive.
In my presence,
You'll melt away and flow.
Oh snow! Oh snow!

When will you come,
When will you go?
Gazing at the sky
I can't help but cry.
The fault in our stars
Can't go away overnight.
Oh snow! I know.
So, let's meet in another life.

~Medoll

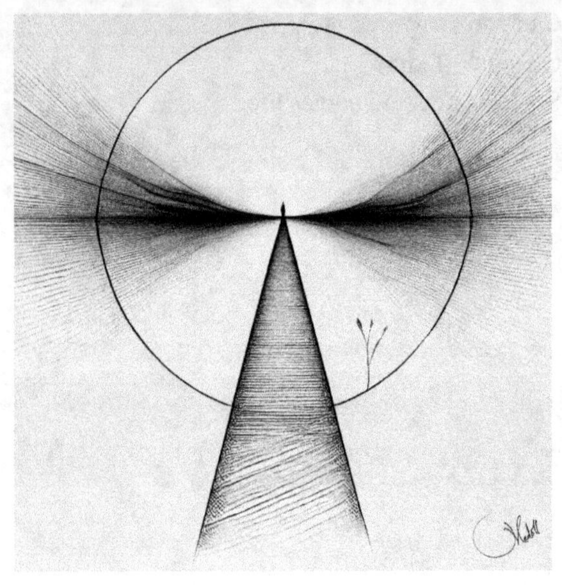

Untold

Heard a lot of noise
While strolling down a lane
A jargon going on—
Did you murmur my name?
A low voice I heard,
That made me shiver to my bones.
A demon in human skin!
Unnatural and uncultured.
A demon is what you assumed me to be?

If you can remember me
I will remain in your memories gratefully
Don't bother if you can't.
I ain't trying to sway your heart,
Just walking on an untold path.
Is there a right or wrong track
If you follow your heart?
Will it lead to the absolute end?
Who cares about the crowded road
I'll walk the single plank bridge
Alone into the dark.

~Medoll

End Game

Purest soul drenches in pain,
While devils smile behind your back.
Is it the time to determine
Affix my path to pursue
My destiny.
If it's meant to be
It will come to me.
I know this much,
From all the learnings
I had in schools of philosophy.
Also the lessons from my own experiences.
I won't tell you when that happens
Whether I'll find success
Or weep over my failures
Let time be the sole judge
Of my life.
Don't interfere,
I beg you,
In the matters of mine.
Let me live
Till Morpheus comes to me
To mark my last second
Until then I will play
My own end game.

~Medoll

Whispers of Fear: Tale of Control

Click!
Echoes fill the air,
Each minute alone,
A suffocating despair.

An eerie presence, unseen,
Lingers with an ever-watchful gaze,
Through keyholes it peers,
My sanctuary ablaze.

No safety in my own abode,
His specter haunts each room,
Chilling whispers, crawling fears,
Like insects in the gloom.

A letter arrives, a vile decree,
My images, a threat's disguise,
To be dissolved in acid's bite,
Should I dare to defy.

Or sliced like mutton, should I dare to smile,
At someone other than he,
I ponder my offense, unknown,
Trapped in this tyranny.

Confined, watched by unseen eyes,
Threatened, as if bereft of life's rights,
His control, a suffocating noose,
Dictating my actions, in darkened rues.

~Medoll

Autumn

You, the universe, my first thought,
Every dawn, in my mind you sought.
My sole companion, day and night,
Every moment with you, pure delight.

From the start, my affection grew,
But your indifference, a bitter brew.
Though cherished, our time together flew,
Yet you couldn't love me through and through.

Each moment, a treasure, with you near,
Touching my soul, drawing me near.
But your coldness, like winter's chill,
Made me shiver, against my will.

Like spring flowers, I bloomed for you,
But in your eyes, no love showed through.
I, a rose in winter's embrace,
Fading, as you turn your face.

You, a pine, oblivious to time,
While I, a leaf, lost in your rhyme.
To you, just a chip, hidden away,
Now I shed you, bid you no stay.

~Medoll

Shadows of Fear: A Voyage Within

Today, fear grips me tight,
Inside my head, a tumultuous fight.
Scared of the feelings I cannot grasp,
Emotions lost, like shadows they clasp.

Your voice echoes loud and clear,
Yet understanding, I cannot steer.
Broken, fragmented, something's awry,
Unable to relate, I question why.

When I gaze upon your face,
No melting heart, no tender embrace.
Tears flow freely for strangers from afar,
But for those close, they're kept behind bars.

Afraid of this emptiness inside,
Scared of the mirror where I hide.
Terrified you'll see my flaws,
As I struggle with my inner wars.

Where can I flee from my own shade,
Long and dark, an endless cascade?
Every word you speak, rings true,
Fears of inadequacy, fears of you.

Anger paints my soul's terrain,
Agitated and annoyed, I remain.
Roaming this land, this tiny plot,
Breathing wasted, feeling caught.

Am I nothing but debris?
Still, I wander, searching to see.
Angels and devils, can they be told apart?
Or am I lost, playing a futile part?

What deeds have I done, who am I?
Lost control as time slips by.
The devil inside, what does it crave?
Scared of myself, when it rises from the grave.

~Medoll

A dive towards dream

So dense, the sea appears
Is there no end
To this misery?
The pain of loneliness
Deepens with each inch
As I dive more
And more
Into the abyss
Underneath the layers
Of this dreadful brook
Am I lost?
I took a quick look around
But each glance says
I can't see farther.
If I must reach to the end
I have to dive till the end
Struggle a little more.

Maybe I am wrong
But even so, I can see the end
Find the pearls and gems
A new world beneath the blue sheet
The thought of it revives me
Anyway I am in no good place
Let's escape this darkness

Rather than a rebound path
Let's follow the chosen route
It may take time
But you surely have a chance
To live the dreams
A world of New Orion.
So dive towards your dream.

~Medoll

Restless

Reaching a destination unknown
I want to reach before dawn
Under the shades of black and blue
Will I reach my dreams soon?
Black sky with sparkling stars
Black eyes with shining spark
When you look back,
Once she was a quirky queen of expression
And now, the queen of dark!
The unending pace of my dreams
Fills me with delight
I will hold onto the moments
And let the glee shine through my tears in eyes
Hoping for a journey sublime
Or the restlessness will appear
On the drooling I had the night before
And the nights to come
Spent well in the puzzling stories of muons and
quarks
With your faith by my side
Restlessness will cease disturbing my nights
And the resurgence will add steps to my flight.

~Medoll

I am your Mirror!

I can see it in your eyes
There is so much you hold back
As if there is a story untold
I am certain;
I wasn't delusional this time
But I can see it in your eyes
Either you were testing the waters
Before going down
As if you are afraid of drowning
I am certain;
I wasn't delusional this time
But I can see it in your eyes
Or you were waiting to accept
Yet another failure
As if you were hurt enough
To be numb from the pain
But I can see it in your eyes
The pain isn't gone
It comes back every time
leaving your eyes wet
And red with the fear.
Even if you deny
I can see it in your eyes
Whenever you see me
Find your reflection

Not just your bare body
But search the soul
Never leave its hold
Listen to the heartbeat
Think of what you love the most
Whenever you feel low
Come to me
And see for yourself
That feeling you just encountered
I can see it in your eyes
Sparkling a new-found shine
And your upbeat heart
Never forget that rhythm it brings to your life
Overpowering the outer uproar
With the symphony of your inner core.
Whenever you are in need
Just come to me
To find your reflection
And search your soul.

~Medoll

Beautiful Ending

When the moon turns red,
And the sun turns blue.
That day will come
When time takes its turn
To take away everything
It has given you.

If something fades under sunlight,
It becomes history.
If something gets bathed in the moonlight,
It becomes a myth.
Is it your choice
To pick one over the other?
Or is it your fate
To become ash in the end?

Perhaps, you are destined
To disappear into the air
Lost from everyone's sight.
But how you remain
In the memories of some
That's what makes you eternal.
Even after generations have passed
You may be living
In someone else's heart.

Seeing the world again
Through their eyes.
Learning the meaning of life
From your journey
They may exclaim
"Oh, so that's how it's done."
Acknowledging your inspiring essence,
A brilliant mind, a courageous soul.

So, be greedy once in a while.
Chase the dream you want to realize.
Live a life of your own choice.
Create moments
And let them dry in the bright sunlight.
Save those memories
And let them get bathed in the sheer moonlight.
So when that time comes
You can go with a smile in your eyes,
Leaving behind both history and myth.
A story, one of its own kind.
Accomplishing truly a beautiful ending!

~Medoll